C'EST LA CONFIANCE

C'EST LA CONFIANCE

ON CONFIDENCE IN THE MERCIFUL LOVE OF GOD

APOSTOLIC EXHORTATION

For the 150th Anniversary of the Birth of St. Thérèse of the Child Jesus and the Holy Face

POPE FRANCIS

Our Sunday Visitor
Huntington, Indiana

Published 2023 by Our Sunday Visitor
29 28 27 26 25 24 23 1 2 3 4 5 6 7 8 9

Our Sunday Visitor Publishing Division,
Our Sunday Visitor, Inc., 200 Noll Plaza,
Huntington, IN 46750;
1-800-348-2440; www.osv.com.

ISBN: 978-1-63966-237-1 (Inventory No. T2917)
eISBN: 978-1-63966-238-8

Cover design: Tyler Ottinger
Cover art: AdobeStock
Interior design: Amanda Falk

Printed in the United States of America

C'EST LA CONFIANCE

1. *"C'est la confiance et rien que la confiance qui doit nous conduire à l'Amour."* "It is confidence and nothing but confidence that must lead us to Love."[1]

2. These striking words of St. Thérèse of the Child Jesus and the Holy Face say it all. They sum up the genius of her spirituality and would suffice to justify the fact that she has been named a Doctor of the Church. Confidence, "nothing but confidence," is the sole path that leads us to the Love that grants everything. With confidence, the wellspring of grace overflows into our lives, the Gospel takes flesh within us and makes us channels of mercy for our brothers and sisters.

3. It is confidence that sustains us daily and will enable us to stand before the Lord on the day when he calls us to himself: "In the evening of this life, I shall appear before you with empty hands, for I do not ask you, Lord, to count my works. All our justice is stained in your eyes. I wish, then, to be clothed in your own *Justice* and to receive from your *Love* the eternal possession of *yourself*."[2]

4. Saint Thérèse is one of the best-known and most beloved saints in our world. Like St. Francis of Assisi, she is loved by non-Christians and nonbelievers as well. In addition, she has been recognized by UNESCO as one of the most significant figures for contemporary humanity.[3] We would do well to delve more deeply into her message as we commemorate the 150th anniversary of her birth in Alençon (January 2, 1873) and the centenary of her beatification.[4] Yet I have not chosen to issue this exhortation on either of those dates, or on her liturgical memorial, so that this message may transcend those celebrations and be taken up as part of the spiritual treasury of the Church. Its publication on the liturgical memorial of St. Teresa of Ávila is a way of presenting St. Thérèse of the Child Jesus and the Holy Face as the mature fruit of the reform of the Carmel and of the spirituality of the great Spanish saint.

5. The earthly life of Saint Thérèse was brief, a mere twenty-four years, and completely ordinary, first in her family and then in the Carmel of Lisieux. The extraordinary burst of light and love that

she radiated came to be known soon after her death, with the publication of her writings and thanks to the countless graces bestowed on the faithful who invoked her intercession.

6. The Church quickly recognized her great significance and the distinctiveness of her evangelical spirituality. Thérèse met Pope Leo XIII during a pilgrimage to Rome in 1887 and asked his permission to enter the Carmel at the age of fifteen. Not long after her death, Saint Pius X, sensing her spiritual grandeur, stated that she would become the greatest saint of modern times. Thérèse was declared "Venerable" in 1921 by Pope Benedict XV, who, in praising her virtues, saw them embodied in her "little way" of spiritual childhood.[5] She was beatified a century ago and then canonized on May 17, 1925, by Pope Pius XI, who thanked the Lord for granting that she be the first "Blessed" whom he raised to the honor of the altars and the first saint whom he canonized.[6] In 1927, the same pope declared her the Patroness of the Missions.[7] Thérèse was proclaimed one of the patron saints of France in 1944 by Venerable Pius XII,[8] who on

several occasions developed the theme of spiritual childhood.[9] Saint Paul VI liked to recall that he was baptized on September 30, 1897, the day of her death, and on the centenary of her birth he wrote a letter on her teaching to the bishop of Bayeux and Lisieux.[10] On June 2, 1980, during his first apostolic journey to France, Saint John Paul II visited the basilica dedicated to her, and in 1997 declared her a Doctor of the Church.[11] He also referred to Thérèse as "an expert in the *scientia amoris*."[12] Pope Benedict XVI returned to the subject of her "science of love" and proposed it as "a guide for all, especially those in the People of God who carry out their ministry as theologians."[13] Finally, in 2015, I had the joy of canonizing her parents, Louis and Zélie, during the Synod on the Family. More recently, I devoted one of my weekly General Audience talks to Saint Thérèse, as part of a cycle of catecheses on apostolic zeal.[14]

1. Jesus for others

7. In the name that Thérèse chose as a religious, Jesus stands out as the "Child" who manifests the mystery of the Incarnation, and the "Holy Face" of the one who surrendered himself completely on the cross. She is "St. Thérèse of the Child Jesus and the Holy Face."

8. The name of Jesus was constantly on her lips, as an act of love, even to her last breath. She had also written these words in her cell: "Jesus is my one love." It was her interpretation of the supreme statement of the New Testament: "God is love" (1 Jn 4:8, 16).

A MISSIONARY SOUL

9. As with every authentic encounter with Christ, this experience of faith summoned her to mission. Thérèse could define her mission in these words: "I shall desire in heaven the same thing as I do now on earth: to love Jesus and to make him loved."[15] She wrote that she entered Carmel "to save souls."[16] In a word, she

did not view her consecration to God apart from the pursuit of the good of her brothers and sisters. She shared the merciful love of the Father for his sinful son and the love of the Good Shepherd for the sheep who were lost, astray, and wounded. For this reason, Thérèse is the patroness of the missions and a model of evangelization.

10. The final pages of her *Story of a Soul*[17] are a missionary testament. They express her appreciation of the fact that evangelization takes place by attraction,[18] not by pressure or proselytism. It is worthwhile reading her own words in this regard: "*Draw me, we shall run after you in the odor of your ointments.* O Jesus! It is not even necessary to say: *When drawing me, draw the souls whom I love!* This simple statement, 'Draw me,' suffices. I understand, Lord, that when a soul allows herself to be captivated by *the odor of your ointments*, she cannot run alone; all the souls whom she loves follow in her train; this is done without constraint, without effort, it is a natural consequence of her attraction for you. Just as a torrent, throwing itself with impetuosity into the ocean,

drags after it everything it encounters in its passage, in the same way, O Jesus, the soul who plunges into the shoreless ocean of your Love, draws with her all the treasures she possesses. Lord, you know it, I have no other treasures than the souls it has pleased you to unite to mine."[19]

11. In this passage, Thérèse quotes the words of the bride to the bridegroom in the Song of Songs (cf. 1:3–4), following the profound interpretation found in the writings of the Doctors of Carmel, St. Teresa of Ávila and St. John of the Cross. The bridegroom is Jesus, the Son of God who united himself to our humanity in the Incarnation and redeemed it on the cross. There, from his open side, he gave birth to the Church, his beloved bride, for which he gave his life (cf. Eph 5:25). What is striking is that Thérèse, conscious of her own impending death, did not approach this mystery merely as a source of personal consolation, but in a fervent apostolic spirit.

THE GRACE THAT SETS US FREE FROM SELF-ABSORPTION

12. We see something similar when Thérèse

speaks of the working of the Holy Spirit, which immediately takes on a missionary hue: "That is my prayer. I ask Jesus to draw me to the flames of his love, to unite me so closely to him that he live and act in me. I feel that the more the fire of love burns within my heart, the more I shall say, '*Draw me*': the more also the souls who will approach me (poor little piece of iron, useless if I withdraw from the divine furnace), the more these souls *will run swiftly in the odor of the ointments of their Beloved*, for a soul that is burning with love cannot remain inactive."[20]

13. In the heart of Thérèse, the grace of baptism became this impetuous torrent flowing into the ocean of Christ's love and dragging in its wake a multitude of brothers and sisters. This is what happened, especially after her death. It was her promised "shower of roses."[21]

2. The little way of trust and love

14. One of the most important insights of Thérèse for the benefit of the entire People of God is her "little way," the path of trust and love, also known as *the way of spiritual childhood*. Everyone can follow this way, whatever their age or state in life. It is the way that the heavenly Father reveals to the little ones (cf. Mt 11:25).

15. In the *Story of a Soul*,[22] Thérèse tells how she discovered the little way: "I can, then, in spite of my littleness, aspire to holiness. It is impossible for me to grow up, and so I must bear with myself such as I am, with all my imperfections. But I want to seek out a means of going to heaven by a little way, a way that is very straight, very short, and totally new."[23]

16. To describe that way, she uses the image of an elevator: "The elevator which must raise me to heaven is your arms, O Jesus! And for this, I had no need to grow

up, but rather I had to remain *little* and become this more and more."[24] Little, incapable of being confident in herself, and yet firmly secure in the loving power of the Lord's arms.

17. This is the "sweet way of love"[25] that Jesus sets before the little and the poor, before everyone. It is the way of true happiness. In place of a Pelagian notion of holiness,[26] individualistic and elitist, more ascetic than mystical, that primarily emphasizes human effort, Thérèse always stresses the primacy of God's work, his gift of grace. As a result, she could say: "I always feel, however, the same bold confidence of becoming a great saint, because I don't count on my merits, since I have *none*, but I trust in him who is Virtue and Holiness. God alone, content with my weak efforts, will raise me to himself and make me a *saint*, clothing me in his infinite merits."[27]

APART FROM ALL MERIT

18. This way of speaking is in no way opposed to the traditional Catholic teaching on the increase of grace — namely, that once gratuitously justified by sanctifying

grace, we are changed and enabled to cooperate by our good works in a process of growth in holiness. Through this "elevation" we can possess real merits by virtue of the development of the grace received.

19. Thérèse, for her part, wished to highlight the primacy of God's action; she encourages us to have complete confidence as we contemplate the love of Christ poured out to the end. At the heart of her teaching is the realization that, since we are incapable of being certain about ourselves,[28] we cannot be sure of our merits. Hence, it is not possible to trust in our own efforts or achievements. The Catechism of the Catholic Church chose to quote the words that Saint Thérèse addressed to the Lord: "I will appear before you with empty hands,"[29] in order to express that "the saints have always had a lively awareness that their merits were pure grace."[30] This conviction gives rise to a joyful and tender gratitude.

20. It is most fitting, then, that we should place heartfelt trust not in ourselves but in the infinite mercy of a God who loves us unconditionally and has already giv-

en us everything in the Cross of Jesus Christ.[31] For this reason, Thérèse never uses the expression, common enough in her day, "I will become a saint."

21. Even so, her boundless confidence encourages all who feel frail, limited, and sinful to let themselves be elevated and transformed in order to reach greater heights. "If all weak and imperfect souls felt what the least of souls feels — that is, the soul of your little Thérèse — not one would despair of reaching the summit of the mount of love. Jesus does not demand great actions from us, but simply *surrender* and *gratitude*."[32]

22. This insistence of Thérèse on God's initiative leads her, when speaking of the Eucharist, to put first not her desire to receive Jesus in holy Communion, but rather the desire of Jesus to unite himself to us and to dwell in our hearts.[33] In her *Act of Oblation to Merciful Love*, saddened by her inability to receive Communion each day, she tells Jesus, "Remain in me as in a tabernacle."[34] Her gaze remained fixed not on herself and her own needs but on Christ, who loves, seeks, desires, and dwells within.

DAILY ABANDONMENT

23. The confidence that Thérèse proposes has to do with more than our individual sanctification and salvation. It has an integral meaning that embraces the totality of concrete existence and finds application in our daily lives, where we are often assailed by fears, the desire for human security, the need to have everything under control. Here we see the importance of her invitation to a holy "abandonment."

24. The complete confidence that becomes an abandonment in Love sets us free from obsessive calculations, constant worry about the future, and fears that take away our peace. In her final days, Thérèse insisted on this: "We who run in the way of love shouldn't be thinking of suffering that can take place in the future; it's a lack of confidence."[35] If we are in the hands of a Father who loves us without limits, this will be the case come what may; we will be able to move beyond whatever may happen to us and, in one way or another, his plan of love and fullness will come to fulfilment in our lives.

FIRE BURNING IN THE NIGHT

25. Thérèse experienced faith most powerfully and surely in the midst of the dark night and especially amid the darkness of Calvary. Her witness culminated in the final months of her life, in the great "trial against the faith"[36] that began at Easter 1896. In her account,[37] she directly relates this period of testing to the painful reality of the atheism of her time. The last years of the nineteenth century were the "golden age" of modern atheism as a philosophical and ideological system. When she wrote that Jesus allowed her soul "to be invaded by the thickest darkness,"[38] she was evoking the darkness of atheism and the rejection of the Christian faith. In union with Jesus, who took upon himself all the darkness of the sin of the world when he willed to drink from the cup of the Passion, Thérèse came to appreciate its underlying sense of despair and sheer emptiness.[39]

26. Yet darkness cannot overcome the light: Thérèse had been conquered by the One who came as light into the world (cf. Jn 12:46).[40] Her account reveals the heroic nature of her faith, her triumph in

spiritual combat with the most powerful temptations. She felt herself a sister to atheists, seated with them at table, like Jesus who sat with sinners (cf. Mt 9:10–13). She interceded for them, ever renewing her own act of faith, in constant loving communion with the Lord: "I run toward my Jesus. I tell him I am ready to shed my blood to the last drop to profess faith in the existence of *heaven*. I tell him, too, that I am happy not to enjoy this beautiful heaven on this earth so that he will open it for all eternity to poor unbelievers."[41]

27. Together with faith, Thérèse experienced a deep and boundless trust in God's infinite mercy, "confidence that must lead us to Love."[42] Even in her darkness, she experienced the complete trust of a child that finds refuge, unafraid, in the embrace of its father and mother. For Thérèse, the one God is revealed above all else in his mercy, which is the key to understanding everything else that can be said of him: "To me he has granted his *infinite mercy* and *through it* I contemplate and adore the other divine perfections! All of these perfections appear to be resplendent *with love*, even his justice (and

perhaps this even more so than the others) seems to me clothed in *love*."[43] This is one of the loftiest insights of Thérèse, one of her major contributions to the entire People of God. In an extraordinary way, she probed the depths of divine mercy, and drew from them the light of her limitless hope.

A MOST FIRM HOPE

28. Before entering the Carmel, Thérèse had felt a remarkable spiritual closeness to one of the most unfortunate of men, the criminal Henri Pranzini, sentenced to death for a triple murder for which he was unrepentant.[44] By having Masses offered for him and praying with complete confidence for his salvation, she was convinced that she was drawing him ever closer to the blood of Jesus, and she told God that she was sure that at the last moment he would pardon him, "even if he went to his death without *any signs of repentance*." As the reason for her certainty, she stated, "I was absolutely confident in the mercy of Jesus."[45] How great was her emotion when she learned that Pranzini, after mounting the scaffold, "suddenly, seized by an inspiration, turned, took hold of

the *crucifix* the priest was holding out to him and *kissed* the *sacred wounds three times!*"[46] This intense experience of hoping against all hope proved fundamental for her: "After this unique grace, my desire to save souls grows each day."[47]

29. Thérèse was conscious of the tragic reality of sin, yet she remained constantly immersed in the mystery of Christ, certain that "where sin increased, grace abounded all the more" (Rom 5:20). The sin of the world is great but not infinite, whereas the merciful love of the Redeemer is indeed infinite. Thérèse testifies to the definitive victory of Jesus, through his passion, death, and resurrection, over all the powers of evil. Filled with confidence, she dared to explain: "Jesus, allow me to save very many souls; let no soul be lost today. … Jesus, pardon me if I say anything I should not say. I only want to give you joy and to console you."[48] This now leads us to consider another aspect of the breath of fresh air that is the message of St. Thérèse of the Child Jesus and the Holy Face.

3. I will be love

30. As "greater" than faith and hope, charity will never pass away (cf. 1 Cor 13:8–13). It is the supreme gift of the Holy Spirit and "the mother and the root of all the virtues."[49]

CHARITY AS A PERSONAL ATTITUDE OF LOVE

31. The *Story of a Soul* is a testimonial to charity, in which Thérèse offers us a commentary on Jesus' new commandment: "that you love one another as I have loved you" (Jn 15:12).[50] Jesus thirsts for this response to his love. Indeed, he "did not fear to *beg* for a little water from the Samaritan woman. He was thirsty. But when he said, 'Give me to drink,' it was the *love* of his poor creature that the Creator of the universe was seeking. He was thirsty for love."[51] Thérèse wished to respond to the love of Jesus, to offer him love in return for love.[52]

32. The symbolism of spousal love emphasizes the mutual self-gift of the bridegroom

and the bride. Thus, inspired by the Song of Songs 2:16, Thérèse writes, "I think that the Heart of my Spouse is mine alone, just as mine is his alone, and I speak to him then in the solitude of this delightful heart to heart, while waiting to contemplate him one day face to face."[53] Although the Lord loves us together as a people, at the same time charity works in a most personal way: "heart to heart."

33. Thérèse possessed complete certainty that Jesus loved her and knew her personally at the time of his passion: "He loved me and gave himself for me" (Gal 2:20). As she contemplated Jesus in his agony, she told him, "You saw me."[54] In the same way, she said to the Child Jesus in the arms of his mother, "With your little hand that caressed Mary, you upheld the world and gave it life, and you thought of me."[55] So, too, at the beginning of the *Story of a Soul*, she contemplated the love of Jesus for all humanity and for each individual, as if he or she were the only one in the world.[56]

34. The act of love — repeating the words, "Jesus I love you" — which became as

natural to Thérèse as breathing, is the key to her understanding of the Gospel. With that love, she immersed herself in all the mysteries of the life of Christ, making herself his contemporary and placing herself within the Gospel together with Mary and Joseph, Mary Magdalene, and the apostles. Together with them, she penetrated to the depths of the love of the heart of Jesus. Let us take one example: "When I see Magdalene walking up before the many guests, washing with her tears the feet of her adored Master, whom she is touching for the first time, I feel that *her heart* has understood the abysses of love and mercy *of the Heart of Jesus*, and, sinner though she is, this Heart of love was not only disposed to pardon her, but to lavish on her the blessings of divine intimacy, to lift her to the highest summits of contemplation."[57]

THE GREATEST LOVE IN SUPREME SIMPLICITY

35. At the end of the *Story of a Soul*, Thérèse presents us with her Act of Oblation to Merciful Love.[58] Once she surrendered completely to the working of the Spirit, she received, quietly and unob-

trusively, an abundant outpouring of living water: "rivers, or better, the oceans of graces that flooded my soul."[59] This is the mystical life that, apart from any extraordinary phenomena, offers itself to all the faithful as a daily experience of love.

36. Thérèse practiced charity in littleness, in the simplest things of daily life, and she did so in the company of the Virgin Mary, from whom she learned that "*to love is to give everything. It's to give oneself.*"[60] While preachers in those days often celebrated Mary's grandeur in ways that made her seem far removed from us, Thérèse showed, starting with the Gospel, that Mary is the greatest in the kingdom of heaven because she is the least (cf. Mt 18:4), the one closest to Jesus in his abasement. She saw that, if the apocrypha are full of striking and amazing feats, the Gospels show us a lowly and poor life lived in the simplicity of faith. Jesus himself wanted Mary to be the example of a soul that seeks him with a simple faith.[61] Mary was the first to experience the "little way" in pure faith and humility. Consequently, Thérèse did not hesitate to write:

Mother full of grace, I know that
in Nazareth
You live in poverty, wanting
nothing more.
No rapture, miracle or ecstasy
Embellish your life, O Queen of
the Elect! …
The number of little ones on
earth is truly great.
They can raise their eyes to you
without trembling.
It's by the ordinary way, incompa-
rable Mother,
That you like to walk to guide
them to heaven.[62]

37. Thérèse does tell us of certain moments of grace experienced amid the simplicity of daily life, like the sudden insight she had when accompanying a sick and somewhat irascible sister. Even so, those experiences of a more intense charity came about in the most ordinary ways: "One winter night I was carrying out my little duty as usual; it was cold, it was night. Suddenly I heard off in the distance the harmonious sound of a musical instrument. I then pictured a well-lighted drawing room, brilliantly gilded,

filled with elegantly dressed young ladies conversing together and conferring upon each other all sorts of compliments and other worldly remarks. Then my glance fell upon the poor invalid whom I was supporting. Instead of the beautiful strains of music I heard only her occasional complaints, and instead of the rich gildings I saw only the bricks of our austere cloister, hardly visible in the glimmering light. I cannot express in words what happened in my soul; what I know is that the Lord illumined it with rays of truth, which so far surpassed the dark brilliance of earthly feasts that I could not believe my happiness. Ah! I would not have exchanged the ten minutes employed in carrying out my humble office of charity to enjoy a thousand years of worldly feasts."[63]

IN THE HEART OF THE CHURCH

38. From St. Teresa of Ávila, Thérèse inherited a great love for the Church and was able to plumb the depths of this mystery. We see this in her discovery of the "heart of the Church." In a lengthy prayer to Jesus,[64] written September 8, 1896, the sixth anniversary of her religious profession, the saint confided to the Lord that

she felt driven by an immense desire, a passion for the Gospel that no vocation, by itself, could satisfy. And so, in seeking her "place" in the Church, she turned to chapters twelve and thirteen of the First Letter of Saint Paul to the Corinthians.

39. There, in chapter twelve, the apostle employs the metaphor of the body and its members to explain that the Church embraces a great variety of hierarchically ordered charisms. Yet this description was not enough for Thérèse. She continued her search and read the "hymn to charity" in chapter thirteen. There she came upon the eminent answer to her question and wrote this memorable page: "Considering the mystical body of the Church, I had not recognized myself in any of the members described by Saint Paul, or rather I desired to see myself in them *all*. *Charity* gave me the key to my *vocation*. I understood that if the Church had a body composed of different members, the most necessary and most noble of all could not be lacking to it, and so I understood that *the Church had a Heart, and that this Heart was burning with love. I understood it was love alone* that made the Church's

members act, that if *Love* ever became extinct, apostles would not preach the Gospel and martyrs would not shed their blood. I understood that *Love comprised all vocations, that love was everything, that it embraced all times and places ... in a word: that it was eternal!* Then, in the excess of my delirious joy, I cried out: O Jesus, my Love ... my *vocation*, at last I have found it ... *my vocation is Love*! Yes, I have found my place in the Church, and it is you, O my God, who have given me this place; in the heart of the Church, my Mother, I shall be *Love*. Thus I shall be everything, and thus my dream will be realized."[65]

40. This heart was not that of a triumphalistic Church, but of a loving, humble and merciful Church. Thérèse never set herself above others, but took the lowest place together with the Son of God, who for our sake became a slave and humbled himself, becoming obedient, even to death on a cross (cf. Phil 2:7–8).

41. This discovery of the heart of the Church is also a great source of light for us today. It preserves us from being scan-

dalized by the limitations and weaknesses of the ecclesiastical institution with its shadows and sins and enables us to enter into the Church's "heart burning with love," which burst into flame at Pentecost thanks to the gift of the Holy Spirit. It is that heart whose fire is rekindled with each of our acts of charity. "I shall be love." This was the radical option of Thérèse, her definitive synthesis and her deepest spiritual identity.

A SHOWER OF ROSES

42. After centuries in which countless saints expressed with great fervor and eloquence their desire to "go to heaven," Saint Thérèse could acknowledge, with utter sincerity, "At the time I was having great interior trials of all kinds, even to the point of asking myself whether heaven really existed."[66] At another time, she said, "When I sing of the happiness of heaven and of the eternal possession of God, I feel no joy in this, for I sing simply what *I want to believe.*"[67] What had happened? Thérèse was hearing God's call to put fire into the heart of the Church more than to think of her own personal happiness.

43. The transformation that was taking place enabled her to pass from a fervent desire for heaven to a constant, burning desire for the good of all, culminating in her dream of continuing in heaven her mission of loving Jesus and making him loved. As she wrote in one of her last letters: "I really count on not remaining inactive in heaven. My desire is to work still for the Church and for souls."[68] And in those very days she said, even more directly: "My heaven will be spent on earth until the end of the world. Yes, I want to spend my heaven in doing good on earth."[69]

44. In those words, Thérèse expressed her most assured response to the singular gift that the Lord was granting her, the remarkable light that God was shedding upon her. In this way, she arrived at her ultimate personal synthesis of the Gospel, one that began with complete trust and ended in total abandonment for the sake of others. She had no doubt about the fruitfulness of that abandonment: "I think of all the good that I would like to do after my death."[70] "God would not have given me the desire of doing good

on earth after my death, if he didn't will to realize it."[71] "It will be like a shower of roses."[72]

45. She had come full circle. "*C'est la confiance.*" It is trust that brings us to love and thus sets us free from fear. It is trust that helps us to stop looking to ourselves and enables us to put into God's hands what he alone can accomplish. Doing so provides us with an immense source of love and energy for seeking the good of our brothers and sisters. And so, amid the suffering of her last days, Thérèse was able to say: "*I count only on love.*"[73] In the end, only love counts. Trust makes roses blossom and pours them forth as an overflow of the superabundance of God's love. Let us ask, then, for such trust as a free and precious gift of grace, so that the paths of the Gospel may open up in our lives.

4. At the heart of the Gospel

46. In *Evangelii Gaudium*, I urged a return to the freshness of the source, in order to emphasize what is essential and indispensable. I now consider it fitting to take up that invitation and propose it anew.

THE DOCTOR OF SYNTHESIS

47. This exhortation on Saint Thérèse allows me to observe that, in a missionary Church, "the message has to concentrate on the essentials, on what is most beautiful, most grand, most appealing, and at the same time most necessary. The message is simplified while losing none of its depth and truth, and thus becomes all the more forceful and convincing."[74] The luminous core of that message is "the beauty of the saving love of God made manifest in Jesus Christ who died and rose from the dead."[75]

48. Not everything is equally central, because there is an order or hierarchy among

the truths of the Church, and "this holds true as much for the dogmas of faith as for the whole corpus of the Church's teaching, including her moral teaching."[76] The center of Christian morality is charity, as our response to the unconditional love of the Trinity. Consequently, "works of love directed towards one's neighbor are the most perfect manifestation of the interior grace of the Spirit."[77] In the end, only love counts.

49. The specific contribution that Thérèse offers us as a saint and a Doctor of the Church is not analytical, along the lines, for example, of St. Thomas Aquinas. Her contribution is more synthetic, for her genius consists in leading us to what is central, essential, and indispensable. By her words and her personal experience, she shows that, while it is true that all the Church's teachings and rules have their importance, their value, their clarity, some are more urgent and more foundational for the Christian life. That is where Thérèse directed her eyes and her heart.

50. As theologians, moralists, and spiritual writers, as pastors and as believers,

wherever we find ourselves, we need constantly to appropriate this insight of Thérèse and to draw from it consequences both theoretical and practical, doctrinal and pastoral, personal and communal. We need boldness and interior freedom to do so.

51. At times, the only quotes we find cited from this saint are secondary to her message, or deal with things she has in common with any other saint, such as prayer, sacrifice, Eucharistic piety, and any number of other beautiful testimonies. Yet in this way, we could be depriving ourselves of what is most specific about her gift to the Church. We forget that "each saint is a mission, planned by the Father to reflect and embody, at a specific moment in history, a certain aspect of the Gospel."[78] Indeed, "to recognize the word that the Lord wishes to speak to us through one of his saints, we do not need to get caught up in details. … What we need to contemplate is the totality of their life, their entire journey of growth in holiness, the reflection of Jesus Christ that emerges when we grasp their overall meaning as a person."[79] This is all the more true in the

case of Saint Thérèse, since we are dealing with a "Doctor of synthesis."

52. From heaven to earth, the timely witness of St. Thérèse of the Child Jesus and the Holy Face endures in all the grandeur of her little way.

In an age that urges us to focus on ourselves and our own interests, Thérèse shows us the beauty of making our lives a gift.

At a time when the most superficial needs and desires are glorified, she testifies to the radicalism of the Gospel.

In an age of individualism, she makes us discover the value of a love that becomes intercession for others.

At a time when human beings are obsessed with grandeur and new forms of power, she points out to us the little way.

In an age that casts aside so many of our brothers and sisters, she teaches us the beauty of concern and responsibility for one another.

At a time of great complexity, she can help us rediscover the importance of simplicity, the absolute primacy of love, trust, and abandonment, and thus move beyond a legalistic or moralistic mindset that would fill the Christian life with rules and regulations, and cause the joy of the Gospel to grow cold.

In an age of indifference and self-absorption, Thérèse inspires us to be missionary disciples, captivated by the attractiveness of Jesus and the Gospel.

53. A century and a half after her birth, Thérèse is more alive than ever in the pilgrim Church, in the heart of God's people. She accompanies us on our pilgrim way, doing good on earth, as she had so greatly desired. The most lovely signs of her spiritual vitality are the innumerable "roses" that Thérèse continues to strew: the graces God grants us through her loving intercession in order to sustain us on our journey through life.

Dear Saint Thérèse,
the Church needs to radiate the
  brightness,

the fragrance and the joy of the
Gospel.
Send us your roses!
Help us to be, like yourself,
ever confident in God's immense love for us,
so that we may imitate each day
your "little way" of holiness.
Amen.

Given in Rome, in the Basilica of St. John Lateran, on October 15, the Memorial of Saint Teresa of Ávila, in the year 2023, the eleventh of my pontificate.

FRANCIS

NOTES

1. St. Thérèse of the Child Jesus and the Holy Face, Letter 197 to Sister Marie of the Sacred Heart (September 17, 1896): *Letters II*, p. 1000. The English citations of the saint's writings are taken from the translations of her works published by the Institute of Carmelite Studies (ICS), Washington, D.C.: *Story of a Soul* (1996); *Letters I: 1877–1890* (1996); *Letters II: 1890–1897* (1988); *Prayers* (1997); *Poetry* (1996); *Her Last Conversations* (1977).

2. Prayer 6, Act of Oblation to Merciful Love (June 9, 1895): *Prayers*, p. 54; *Story of a Soul*, pp. 276–277.

3. For the two-year period 2022–23, UNESCO recognized Saint Thérèse as a person to be celebrated on the 150th anniversary of her birth.

4. April 29, 1923.

5. Cf. *Decretum super Virtutibus* (August 14, 1921): AAS 13 (1921), 449–452.

6. *Homily for the Canonization* (May 17, 1925): AAS 17 (1925), 211.

7. Cf. AAS 20 (1928), 147–148.

8. Cf. AAS 36 (1944), 329–330.

9. Cf. Pius XII, *Letter to Msgr. François-Marie Picaud, bishop of Bayeux and Lisieux* (August 7, 1947); *Radio Message for the Consecration of the Basilica of Lisieux* (July 11, 1954): AAS 46 (1954), 404–407.

10. Cf. *Letter to Msgr. Jean-Marie-Clément Badré, bishop of Bayeux and Lisieux on the occasion of the Centenary of the Birth of St. Thérèse of the Child Jesus* (January 2, 1973): AAS 65 (1973), 12–15.

11. Cf. AAS 90 (1998), 409–413, 930–944.

12. Apostolic letter *Novo Millennio Ineunte* (January 6, 2001), 42: AAS 93 (2001), 296.

13. *Catechesis* (April 6, 2011), *L'Osservatore Romano* (April 7, 2011), 8.

14. *Catechesis* (June 7, 2023), *L'Osservatore Romano* (June 7, 2023), 2–3.

15. Letter 220 to l'Abbé Bellière (February 24, 1897), *Letters II*, p. 1060.

16. Ms A, 69v: *Story of a Soul*, p. 149.

17. Cf. Ms C, 33v-37r: *Story of a Soul*, pp. 253–259.

18. Cf. Apostolic exhortation *Evangelii Gaudium* (November 24, 2013), 14, 264: AAS 105 (2013), 1025–1026.

19. Ms C, 34r: *Story of a Soul*, p. 254.

20. Ibid., 36r:, *Story of a Soul*, p. 257.

21. *Last Conversations, Yellow Notebook* (June 9, 1897, 3), p. 62.

22. Cf. Ms C, 2v-3r: *Story of a Soul*, pp. 207–208.

23. Ibid., 2v: p. 207.

24. Ibid., 3r: p. 208.

25. Cf. Ms A, 84v: p. 181.

26. Cf. Apostolic exhortation *Gaudete et Exsultate* (March 19, 2018), 47–62: AAS 110 (2018), 1124–1129.

27. Ms A, 32r: *Story of a Soul*, p. 72.

28. This was explained by the Council of Trent: "Whoever considers himself, his personal weakness, and his lack of disposition may fear and tremble about his own grace" (*Decree on Justification*, IX: DS 1534). It is taken up by the Catechism of the Catholic Church, which teaches that it is not possible to have certitude by looking to ourselves or our own actions (cf. No. 2005). The certitude born of trust does not come from ourselves, nor can our own consciousness ground that security, which is not based on introspection. In the words of Saint Paul: "I do not judge myself. I am not aware of anything against myself, but I am not thereby acquitted. It is the Lord who judges me" (1 Cor 4:3–4). St. Thomas Aquinas explains it in the following way: since grace "does not perfectly heal man" (ST I–II, q. 109, art. 9, ad 1), "in the intellect there remains the darkness of ignorance" (ibid., resp.).

29. Prayer 6: *Prayers*, p. 54.

30. Catechism of the Catholic Church, 2011.

31. This was also clearly stated by the Council of Trent: "No devout man should doubt God's mercy"

(*Decree on Justification*, IX: DS 1534); "All should place their firmest hope in God's help" (ibid., XIII: DS 1541).

32. Ms B, 1v: *Story of a Soul*, p. 188.

33. Cf. Ms A, 48v: *Story of a Soul*, pp. 104–105; Letter 92 to Marie Guérin (May 30, 1889): *Letters I*, pp. 567–569.

34. Prayer 6 (June 9, 1895): *Story of a Soul*, p. 276.

35. *Last Conversations, Yellow Notebook* (July 23, 1897, 3): p. 106.

36. Ms C, 31r: *Story of a Soul*, p. 250.

37. Cf. Ms C, 5r-7v: *Story of a Soul*, pp. 211–214.

38. Cf. ibid., 5v: *Story of a Soul*, p. 211.

39. Cf. ibid., 6v: *Story of a Soul*, p. 213.

Cf. Encyclical *Lumen Fidei* (June 29, 2013), 17: AAS 105 (2013), 564–565.

41. Ms C, 7r: *Story of a Soul*, pp. 213–214.

42. Cf. Letter 197 to Sister Marie of the Sacred Heart (September 17, 1896): *Letters II*, p. 1000.

43. Ms A, 83v: *Story of a Soul*, p. 180.

44. Cf. Ms A, 45v–46v: *Story of a Soul*, pp. 98–101.

45. Ibid., 46r: *Story of a Soul*, p. 100.

46. Ibid.

47. Ibid., 46v: *Story of a Soul*, p. 100.

48. Prayer 2 (September 8, 1890): *Prayers*, p. 38.

49. *Summa Theologiae*, I–II, q. 62, art. 4.

50. Cf. Ms C, 11v–31r: *Story of a Soul*, pp. 219–250.

51. Ms B, 1v: *Story of a Soul*, p. 189.

52. Cf. Ms B, 4r: *Story of a Soul*, p. 195.

53. Letter 122 to Céline (October 14, 1890): *Letters II*, p. 709.

54. PN [Poem Number] 24, 21: *Poetry*, p. 128.

55. PN 24, 6: Ibid., p. 124.

56. Cf. Ms A, 3r: *Story of a Soul*, pp. 14–15.

57. Letter 247 to l'Abbé Bellière (June 21, 1897): *Letters II*, p. 1133.

58. Cf. Prayer 6: *Prayers*, pp. 53–55; *Story of a Soul*, pp. 276–277.

59. Ms A, 84r: *Story of a Soul*, p. 181.

60. PN 54, 22: *Poetry*, p. 219.

61. PN 54, 15: Ibid., p. 218.

62. PN 54, 17: Ibid., p. 218.

63. Ms C, 29v–30r: *Story of a Soul*, pp. 248–249.

64. Cf. Ms B, 2r–5v: *Story of a Soul*, pp. 190–200.

65. Ms B, 3v: Ibid., p. 194.

66. Ms A, 80v: *Story of a Soul*, p. 173. This was not a lack of faith. St. Thomas Aquinas taught that in faith, both the intelligence and the will are operative. The adherence of the will can be very solid and well rooted, while the intelligence can be darkened. Cf. *De Veritate* 14,1.

67. Ms C, 7v: *Story of a Soul*, p. 214.

68. Letter 254 to Père Adolphe Roulland (July 14, 1897): *Letters II*, p. 1142.

69. *Last Conversations, Yellow Notebook* (July 17, 1897), p. 102.

70. Ibid. (July 13, 1897, 17), p. 102.

71. Ibid. (July 18, 1897, 1), p. 102.

72. *Last Conversations, Yellow Notebook* (June 9, 1897, 3), p. 62.

73. Letter 242 to Sister Marie of the Trinity (June 6, 1897): *Letters II*, p. 1121.

74. *Evangelii Gaudium*, 35: AAS 105 (2013), 1034.

75. Ibid., 36: AAS 105 (2013), 1035.

76. Ibid.

77. Ibid., 37: AAS 105 (2013), 1035.

78. *Gaudete et Exsultate*, 19: AAS 110 (2018), 1117.

79. Ibid., 22: AAS 110 (2018), 1117.

You might also like:

St. Therese of Lisieux: Meditations with the Little Flower

by Joseph D. White, PhD

This volume, using a fresh, authoritative translation from the original French, will bring *Story of a Soul* to everyone wishing to understand and profit from Thérèse's precious and simple spirituality.

This book includes:

- One hundred quotations from her writings, with brief meditations from Scripture.
- Insightful topics, including purity, God's will, grace, self-abandonment, and joy.